Ultimate **Nashville**

Business Guide

Ultimate **Nashville**
Business Guide

Ultimate Nashville Business Guide:
Proven Business Lessons From Local Nashville Experts Designed To Help You Build A Successful
Nashville Business (first edition)

Copyright © 2012 by David Dutton

Published by Marketing Matters Media
Nashville, TN

CREDITS:
Cover design by Laura Williams of Jiminate
Interior design by Charles Sutherland

Printed in the United States of America.

ISBN 978-0-9884333-0-4

Special discounts are available in quantity purchases by organizations. Requests for more information can be emailed to support@nashpreneur.com.

*To Ian Miller and all the kids
who have the courage to fight cancer.*

Contents

Dedication   *v*

Acknowledgments   *ix*

Introduction   *xi*

1 How I Turned a $35 Website into a Full-time
Income in 90 Days   1

2 Three Things Every Entrepreneur Should Do -
Before You Start Your Business   9

3 The For, The By, and The Why:
3 Reasons Networking is a Must for Today's Entrepreneur   13

4 Small Business Hiring: Are You Hiring a
Problem or a Solution?   19

5 Success and Branch Management   25

6 The Key to Happiness   29

7 Don't Gimme No Lines and Keep Your Hype to Yourself   33

8 Keys to Unselfish Communication   39

9 Building Meaningful Business Relationships Nashville-style   45

10 Love What You Do   51

11 Investment Rules for Entrepreneurs   55

12 Be Specific When Asking for What You Need   61

13 The Business of Radio   65

14 If You Are Not on the Edge,
You are Taking Up Space Too Much Space   69

15 Where Do Dreams Go To Die - Or Do They?   73

16 Getting It All Done: From Strategy Into Action   77

      Epilogue   *83*

How to Get More From David Dutton   85

Consumer Awareness Guide To Hiring
An Online Marketing Consultant   87

100 Great Places To Market Your Nashville Area Business   95

Client Files: From $300 to $11,800 In 11 Months   101

Bonus Interview With Jeff Livak   103

Will You Do Me A Favor?   111

Acknowledgments

To all of the contributing authors in the book, without you taking time out of your busy schedules to be a part of this awesome and important project, this book would of never happened. Thank you for sharing your time and expertise with the Nashville business community.

To my assistant Anna Cook, thank you for helping me organize this massive project. I could not have done it without your help.

To my marketing buddies and closest friends, Greg Ramsier, Jonathan Taylor, and Scott Smith: Without our marketing discussions, I would not accomplish nearly half as much as I do.

Finally, to my wife Sherry, thank you for allowing me to earn a living through entrepreneurship.

Introduction

Give me six hours to chop down a tree and I will spend the first four sharpening the axe. This is a great quote that is attributed to Abraham Lincoln.

Consider reading this short but powerful book as sharpening your axe. Don't worry; it won't take you six hours to read this book, at least it shouldn't.

Like many of my projects, I started out this project by asking myself, "If my best friend or a family member called to ask me a question about a business topic, what would I share with them?".

The answer to that question is what makes up the content of each chapter in this book. I asked each contributing author the same exact question. I wanted a Nashville business professional to be able to pick up this book, read any chapter, and walk away a better business leader.

To walk away a better business leader, you must apply what you learn. Dale Carnegie said *"Knowledge isn't power until it is applied"*. I encourage you to take at least one idea from the book and apply it in your business. I have found that one idea or thought process can lead to the one major idea that I run with.

Also, to make it easy for you to get help, I have included a section at the beginning of each chapter that shares some information about each contributing author. If you have any questions about any of the chapters in the book, don't hesitate to contact any of the experts in this book.

If you are ready to begin, go ahead and turn the page.

David Dutton

How I Turned A $35 Website Into A Full-time Income In 90 Days

Author Name: David Dutton

Company Name: Nashpreneur.com

Title: Founder

Phone: 615-796-0104

Website: www.Nashpreneur.com

Business Description:
Nashpreneur.com is a Nashville based business blog with posts relating to proven marketing strategies, local entrepreneur interviews, social media and more. Nashpreneur.com also hosts local business events as well.

What would you do in this situation?

Lee is an entrepreneur.

However, Lee has no clients in Nashville. In fact, most people don't even know Lee because he doesn't even belong to any networking groups in the area. Spending a million bucks to rent a billboard on I-40 isn't in the cards either.

What would you advise Lee to do to grow his business?

This is a situation that might be familiar to you if you have ever started a business yourself. Finding customers that is. We have all been there.

If it were me, I would have Lee begin by strategically putting together a twelve-week lead generation campaign consisting of a blog, YouTube videos, and starting his own meet-up group to share his best advice on his expertise.

I would also advise him to compile an education-based guide to contribute to potential prospects who would like to test the waters with him. This way his prospects can get some amazing information on a topic and contact him when they are ready for more.

By doing it in this manner, he becomes a trusted expert instead of a pushy salesman. *We love underdogs but we do business with experts—always remember that.*

Since I know that the timing has to be the right for a client to purchase, I would have Lee send out a weekly email filled with entertaining and informational tips on his expertise to stay in contact with potential clients.

This is a great starting point if he wants to build a successful Nashville career on a budget. He could launch his business for less than a hundred bucks and build up from there.

Actually, this is the exact advice that I offered him when I was standing in the mirror a few months ago, right before I started www.Nashpreneur.com with $35.

Without sharing income specifics, I will tell you that I make a full-time income from Nashpreneur.com. I spent $35 to get the brand established and this all happened in 90 days. You can do the same thing if you follow the steps below, regardless of your industry.

In the following six steps, I am going to share with you how I accomplished this and how you can become the trusted expert in your niche here in Nashville by applying the same principles.

Step One: I chose my market

I decided which market that I wanted to zero in on and wanted give value to. For me, it is the Nashville area business community. I wanted to help fellow professionals further develop and increase their business by using multi-media and technology.

> **Your Action Step:** Decide exactly what you're selling and think about who is most likely to buy. The more specific you are the more precise your action step will be.

For example, a private client of mine desires to market only to high-end home buyers. All of our marketing will be concentrated on attracting that specific crowd.

Step Two: I started blogging

Once I determined my market, I wanted to demonstrate my expertise on the subject of marketing as well as use my blog to generate a steady stream of traffic to my business. I started writing powerful how-to articles on generating more customers and referrals. That is exactly what my target market is searching for.

> **Your Action Step:** Establish a blog and start writing about topics your target market would want to know about. If you are in the financial arena, give tips that people can use to make or save money. If you are a massage therapist, write about the benefits of massage or interview current clients and feature them on your blog. People love stories.

Step Three: I started building a list

People need opportunities to get to know you, like you, and trust you. This takes time. By offering a free giveaway, others can get to know you on their own terms. I started offering a free fifty-four minute audio CD called, "*The Ultimate Nashville Marketing Guide*", which really took off once it was released. It is the only one of its kind in Nashville, which is great because I don't have any competition duplicating my product.

To get your wheels spinning, let me take a local company and give you an example of what I would do if I was handling their multimedia marketing.

In September 2010, one of my dreams came true. I was able to purchase one of my dream cars with cash. It was a 2007 Turbo Charged Saturn Sky Redline (Redline translates to FAST).

Since 2007, I had wanted one. However, I have never had a car payment so I didn't plan on getting one in my thirties. I decided I was going to use my business to raise the money and pay cash. It took me 70 days. How? That is a story for another day.

About a year and a half later, our first daughter Addison was born. Now, if you are a father reading this right now, then you know what is coming. You guessed it! The little two seater doesn't really work legally or otherwise when picking up a newborn from daycare. The car had to go.

I needed a dad-mobile so I decided to buy a truck. One Saturday, Sherry and I pulled into Ford Lincoln of Franklin just to look around. Long story short, within two hours I had officially made the change from "Turbo Charged" to "Dad-Mobile".

The lucky salesman who got me to hand over my money was Michael McLain. Nice, friendly guy. We did the deal and left. While I was there though, he asked when my birthday was. I let him know and that was it.

A month later, I got a call on my birthday from Michael. Completely caught me off guard. He wished me happy birthday and asked how I was enjoying the truck. It was a great call. I thought, " He really didn't have to do that, but nice gesture."

Almost two months later, my phone rang and once again, it's Michael. He asked me how the truck is working and again, I tell him that all is good. This time I thought, "Wow! This is great service." Michael chose to go the extra mile.

I share that story with you because I wanted you to know about an exceptional local company but also to highlight a strength that they could utilize powerfully.

If I were running Ford Lincoln of Franklin, I would create a book on the topic of customer service and give it away to anyone who comes and test drives a car. This gives prospects an extra incentive to come into their doors and also sends a message to their prospects that customer service is important to them.

I hope you understand the power of what you just read. *Any company in Nashville can do the exact same thing.*

> **Your Action Step:** Think about something that you can give away that your prospects would love, but doesn't cost you anything or very little to produce. It might be an e-book, a checklist that people can follow, or even an audio program like mine.

Here are fifteen ideas to jump start your brain:

❖ Give away interviews you have conducted with your best clients and frame them as case studies.

❖ Donate a free ebook on the most frequent, embarrassing mistakes your prospects make when buying X or hiring a (insert whatever industry).

❖ Offer a free audio or video interview where someone interviews you on your expertise.

❖ Put together a FAQ report on the top questions asked in your field.

❖ Assemble a FAQ report on the top questions prospects should be asking.

❖ Tape a series of videos of yourself educating your prospect on a topic. If you are in insurance, for example, demonstrate why buying a certain type of insurance is inadequate and how to choose the correct policy for you.

❖ Give away an educational guide on your expertise. This is powerful because your competition won't know what hit them when you release it.

❖ Create a powerful resource list for your industry. An example would be the list that I created of free and mostly free resources featuring business-related items.

❖ Give away a free chapter of your book if you have written one, which I highly suggest.

❖ Create a fact sheet on specific points that your prospects should know about your topic.

❖ Offer subscriber-only special deals or coupons to your email list subscribers.

❖ Offer a tip of the week on your expertise.

❖ Offer a free trial of your product or service.

❖ Start a newsletter offline or online.

❖ Create a free ecourse to which people could subscribe on a particular topic.

Step Four: I started connecting

Because of my blog and the list I was building, I got the opportunity to meet really dynamic people like Bob Hutchins, owner of Buzzplant.com. Bob created the social media campaigns for huge projects like the Passion of the Christ. We met as a result of Nashpreneur and now have a project we are working on together. Bob is also a contributing author in this book.

> **Your Action Step:** Create a plan to reach out to potential prospects and also to other influencers who deal with your target market as well. Look for ways you both can partner to generate leads for each other.

Step Five: I started speaking

I hired two people to book speaking engagements for me locally. By doing that, I was able to work on other projects at the same time. I was also able to land a nice speaking gig at a local chamber, which led me to new clients.

There is *nothing* better for positioning than getting in front of a group and speaking about your expertise.

> **Your Action Step:** Put together two speaking programs that will engage an audience for approximately twenty to thirty minutes. Next, hire someone or start contacting groups and associations locally and ask to be their featured speaker.

Step Six: I started offering strategy sessions

Because of the actions that I just mentioned, people started contacting me for advice on how to put together automated marketing systems like I use on Nashpreneur.com. As a result, I started doing nineteen dollar personalized strategy sessions for people.

Why nineteen dollars?

I like to use business to raise money for charity, so the nineteen dollars helps raise money for St. Jude Children's Research Hospital, which I am very passionate about.

Your Action Step: Can you offer some sort of free or low cost option so that your prospects can try out your product or service? I have no doubt that you can.

In conclusion, I hope you have been inspired and motivated by my story but more importantly, I hope you go and take action to improve your own business right away. By following this proven formula, you too can find success and make a difference in the lives of people you come in contact with.

Three Things Every Entrepreneur Should Do - Before You Start Your Business

Author Name: Jay Clarke

Company Name: Magazines.com

Title: CEO & President

Phone: 615-778-2101

Website: www.magazines.com

Business Description:
With thousands of magazines and books on sale every day, Magazines.
com offers people a fun, easy way to discover hot new reads and helps them
track magazine subscriptions through outstanding selection, simplicity and
service. Magazines.com is the leading independent magazine subscription
agent serving customers online at Magazines.com and by telephone at
800-MAGAZINES (800-624-2946).

Sometimes the best lessons in growing your business are the hardest ones. Here are a few lessons that I've learned—the hard way—about determining what's important and hiring the right people in my career.

Determine Your Core Values First

Before you sit down to formulate your business plan, write your core values. Your core values—a list of practical and relevant expectations as well as your definition of success—will be critically important to your start-up. Your core values are the foundation of your corporate culture and your corporate culture will inform your brand. So it is of the utmost importance to determine these values first.

Not sure how to determine your core values? My suggestion is to think about the superstars, the "A" players, which you currently work with or have worked with in the past. These would be the folks that you would enthusiastically hire or re-hire for your start-up. Make a list of the character traits and the qualities that cause them to be rock stars. Next, make a list of those from your past that were low performers. This list would be the type of folks that you would want to avoid in your start-up. Then write down the traits and the qualities that kept them from excelling. When you complete your two lists, your core values will "jump off of the page."

One of my favorite business-book authors, James Collins, says this about core values: "A company's practices and strategies should change continually to adapt to a changing world. Its core values should not." Before you do anything else, sit down and take the time to figure out what's most important to you by stating core values.

Make Your First Hires Count

Hiring your first three or four people will also be one of the most important decisions you ever make. Most entrepreneurs start with very little funding and it's tempting to fall in the trap of wanting to hire the first people who say, "Yes." This is a huge mistake because those first team members will do a lot—for better or worse—to determine the fate of your company.

If you make the right hires, choose "A Players," get the culture and fit right in the beginning, your business will almost always go fast and go well. If you settle, it may not destroy your business, but it will make things a lot harder for a long time.

It has been said that poor hiring decisions will cost you up to three times their salary once you let them go and will take up to three years to recover. I have found, personally, that both of those measures are conservative.

Identify Your Vice President of No

One of the most important employees for an entrepreneur to hire both in the short and long term is the person I like to call the "Vice President of No". Most entrepreneurs are not good at saying no. We like to say yes, we like to take risks, we like to go fast, and we've never seen an idea we didn't like.

You need someone that you trust to work alongside you to say 'no' to those things that distract you and keep you from your core business. This is your VP of No. Make sure that he or she is alongside you for all of your important decisions. Let him or her wear the black hat and keep you focused on your mission and vision. It is an overused expression, but "Good is the enemy of great." As an entrepreneur, you will find yourself confronted with lots and lots of "good" opportunities. Run away. Stay focused. I recommend that one of your senior teammates be tasked with saying, "no" to the good things so you can say, "yes" to the great things.

Your core values, your first few hires, and your VP of No will be some of the most important decisions you will ever make. Get them wrong, and it will take time and money to recover. Some start-ups never bounce back from missing these steps. But get them right, and your new enterprise will have a much better chance for success.

The For, the By, and the Why: 3 Reasons Networking is a Must for Today's Entrepreneur

Author Name: Christopher M. Hogan
Company Name: 360 Consulting
Title: Speaker, Business Consultant & Financial Coach
Phone: 615.293.6625
Website: www.Chrishogan360.com

Business Description:
We provide financial and business information to educate, encourage & empower today's business owners. We provide private one-on-one coaching, speaking events, workshops and seminars to all size businesses.

As a financial and business consultant to business owners around the country, I am often asked about the value and priority of networking. I have noticed an alarming trend of networking neglect that has only grown with the financial crisis.

The financial crisis has caused slower sales, layoffs, and revised business strategies. As part of those shifts, business leaders often have to take on additional responsibilities to "keep the train rolling" until we come out of this dark financial tunnel.

In fact, many entrepreneurs and small business owners are successful because they can do it all. They've had to fix the company's first computer. They came up with their own advertising. They kept their own books for a long time.

But that same versatility can cause problems. The ability to do everything doesn't create the necessity to do everything.One must find what roles and responsibilities are necessary for that business leader to take on, especially if the company is facing financial challenges. Networking is one of those.

Many entrepreneurs and business leaders are missing out on the value and necessity of building a networking team around them. This support, education, and consulting network will benefit a business leader in a myriad of ways. Let's be clear, I am not talking about a "chit-chat" group that meets just "to meet." I am talking about connecting with winners, shakers and movers that are focused on making success happen.

Consider these reasons as to why networking can be incredibly valuable to your business and should be worth your effort:

1) The FOR: There is a reason it is called being in business **for** yourself. You are trying to make your vision a reality. And one of the best ways of excelling at any goal is to surround yourself with other like-minded and successful people who can push you to new heights. Iron sharpens iron. If you are networking with people that are pushing the limits and crushing it, then you will want to as well, if only because of the risk of looking inferior and weak (and no one wants to be that person). Being around success makes you want to work just that much harder.

2) The BY: Although you might be in business **for** yourself, you are certainly not in business **by** yourself, even if you happen to be the only employee. Although networking is often seen as a means to gain business, networking contacts can, and in many cases, should become your friends. I have often told my business clients - People that know you can grow you. People who know where you are strong and where you are weak can help refine those qualities. And not just for refining, support alone is necessary to the human condition. We all want and need to be affirmed and pushed at points in our lives. Having trusted peers that you can bounce ideas and thoughts off of is an excellent resource for both you and your business.

Being successful may bring accolades and money, but it can also attract insincere people and "yes" people. We have all seen the "posse" hanging around a successful person. Although we'd love for everyone to have such a cheering section, it's better to have peers that by example and encouragement can push you to reach the next level or goal. A person that wants continued success for you will tell you the honest facts when you need to hear them.

3) The WHY: Why are you in business? Every business requires connections to others, whether they are internal connections - among employees, leadership, etc., or external ones - with clients, customers, suppliers and the like. Every networking contact potentially either meets one of those categories, can connect you with someone, or can teach you or learn from you. Ask yourself which categories your contacts fall into.

Consider these thoughts and begin to connect with like-minded people both within and outside of your industry. I encourage my clients to offer to take a potential networking contact to lunch and find out more about what they are doing and how they are doing it. Be honest. Let them know that you want to learn from them to grow you and your business. Talk about your goals and dreams. The more you talk out loud to others about what you want to accomplish, the more you make yourself accountable.

Remember that trying to be everything to everyone is setting yourself up for failure. Likewise, trying to be everything that you need for yourself as an entrepreneur is also risky. Prioritize your workload and consider networking as a fairly high priority. You have worked hard to get where you are. How much further could you go if you were connected with the right people? Only time will tell the answer to this question.

Action step: Think of five to ten people that you should connect with in the next 30 days. You can set up lunches, coffee meetings or even phone calls with follow-up, in-person meetings, but the important step is to do it. Today.

Small Business Hiring: Are You Hiring A Problem Or A Solution?

Author Name: Jennifer Way

Company Name: Way Solutions

Title: Founder and CEO

Phone: 615.227.4700

Website: www.waysolutions.com

Business Description:
Way Solutions serves Fortune 500 and mid-sized companies across a broad range of industries including high tech, consulting, accounting, entertainment, restaurant, health care, and more. Our clients each have unique talent attraction and retention challenges. We leverage cutting-edge talent philosophies to provide solutions with a focus on improving hiring effectiveness, efficiency, talent development, and retention.

Hiring is especially important for a small business. As a small business owner or entrepreneur, you have to wear a lot of hats but you can't do it all on your own. The quality of the team you put together and their ability to work together will make or break your company. Here are a few rules to hiring that will make your hiring successful.

1. Don't hire your friends. The role of an employee and a friend are very different. Save your friendship and hire someone who is qualified to do the job. Friendship is built on having an equal or level relationship. When you are an employer, you introduce hierarchy to that friendship and it leads to weird dynamics for both parties. Having someone become your boss that is your equal on a friendship level can be awkward.

As an employer you might not want to hurt your friend's feelings, so you might be less likely to ask them to do tasks, address negative behaviors, etc. It just makes it uncomfortable for all involved. It can lead to hurt feelings and can damage your relationship long term. Is that really worth it in the long run?

2. Try before you buy when you can. Start by hiring someone to work on a project-by-project basis. This gives you time to see how they actually perform and whether they would be worth the financial risk of bringing them on board.

3. Spend time thinking of defining a role properly upfront. Separate the role from the person performing the role. In other words, every person has different skills and preferences, but whether someone can or can't do something shouldn't determine whether that task is part of the job or not. Think first about what needs to be done, THEN think about who might be good in the role.

4. Use your smallness to your advantage. Think about what kind of experience you can offer that other companies cannot. Responsibility tends to be handed to people at much lower levels in a small organization, offering the opportunity to gain a deeper level of experience and greater variety in that experience. This can be very attractive to driven, but inexperienced employees. Also, be flexible when you can. Schedules, time off, and hours or other special requests are things that you might be able to accommodate which larger organizations may have a tough time allowing.

5. Sell your culture. Figure out the things that make your culture unique and celebrate them. Culture is a defining factor in attracting top talent, but it might also the biggest factor in being successful in that role. Make sure you are hiring someone who can be successful in your environment.

6. Find creative benefits to offer. Look for things that are valuable to your employees and support your culture. Is innovation important to you? Offer a contest or bonus for the best idea. Award continuing education scholarships to those who are top performers.

7. Remember that not every idea has to cost you money. Employees themselves might be willing to pick up some of the cost if it's attractive enough. Some laundry services will come to the office to pick up laundry or dry cleaning on a weekly basis at a discounted rate or perhaps a massage therapist would set up for a half day per week to give chair massages for a fee. Look for things that make employees want to come to work.

8. Consider hiring interns. Internships are meant to be educational opportunities first and foremost. They cannot replace an actual employee and there are several other criteria you should know about the laws about paid vs. unpaid internships. Do a little research to make sure you're in compliance, but it can be totally worth it. Hiring an intern can be a great way to find and train a future potential employee. Work with your local college career center and they can direct you into their program.

9. Don't waste time in your hiring process. Time is expensive. It's the only resource you can't get back or make more of so use your time wisely. Think about the position up front. What experience differentiates one candidate over another? You should have 2-3 requirements for the position and another 2-3 questions that are key differentiators in mind before you even start looking at resumes.

10. Phone screen the top 6-10 resumes. You can tell a lot from 10-15 minutes on the phone with someone. Interviewing too many people wastes a ton of time and drags out your process. Too many entrepreneurs look over the first few resumes and automatically invite them all in for an interview. Resist the urge. Call the top 6-10 people, narrow it down to the top 3-5, and invite them to an interview.

11. Only interview the top 3-5 candidates. You should invest time only with the top talent you've identified. Ask story-based questions based on scenarios that would likely come up in the daily life of someone in the role for which you're interviewing. Listen to the answer and then ask a couple of follow up questions to probe a bit further and make sure you understand the situation. This will help you predict how this person will perform on the job.

Define your 5-10 areas you want to evaluate and ask each candidate the same questions. This ensures that you get the same information from each person. It's best to compare apples to apples so gathering consistent information from each candidate will make your selection process much easier.

If for some reason, you're not satisfied with any of your first rounds of interviews, go back and rethink your profile. If you're considering a second batch of candidates, only consider those that present stronger than the first batch—anything less is a waste of time.

If you follow these guidelines, your hiring process will be both efficient and effective. Every time you hire someone you are either solving problems or creating them. As a small business owner, you don't have time to have to create more distractions. Make sure you are thorough and hire to solve your problems.

Success And Branch Management

Name: Kevin Long

Title: Branch Manager

Phone: 615-991-9912

Website: www.kevinlong.net

Business Description:
We have two branches in the Nashville area, including Sidco Drive in
Nashville and Country Club Drive in Hendersonville. PrimeLending offers
a wide variety of loan products along with in-house processing and
underwriting. It is our goal to develop strong relationships with each
customer and business partner so that we may offer the best service
available.

Success can be defined in a variety of ways. Success is the achievement of one's aim or goal or it is something that happens as a consequence . . . the outcome or result of uncalculated events. In relation to opening and running an office or branch, however, success can only be achieved through proper preparation, the right employees, efficiency, teamwork, positive attitudes, strong leaders and managers, an environment that embraces change, and ongoing effective communication and problem solving. Yes, the list seems long, but it's certainly attainable.

To ensure the success of opening and running a new branch, planning is the first crucial step. Gathering all of the information needed to get your branch up and running is a must. Assumptions cannot be made as to any of the details. Each company, no matter what industry, will be unique so careful attention to what is required for success in your particular industry is critical. In addition to visiting other successful locations, consulting with well-established professionals in your field could prove extremely valuable.

Hiring the right people from the very beginning is also a critical component to a branch's success. A new office will only be as good as the people working within it. John C. Maxwell, leadership expert and New York Times bestselling author, writes in his book The 17 Indisputable Laws of Teamwork, "You can have a distinct vision, a precise plan, plenty of resources, and incredible leadership, but if you don't have the right people, you're not going to get anywhere."

The right people also need to be empowered with proper support. Providing training to develop job specific skills, to increase product knowledge, and to understand company processes and procedures will enable employees to make valuable contributions that lead to success. A successful office will have established systems that promote efficiency, teamwork, and positive attitudes for its employees.

Additionally, the right people must have the right manager. Managing a branch is a large task-- it calls for a solid leader who is willing to be held accountable, takes pride in his or her office and employees, focuses on driving new business, holds a high level of confidence, and understands how to integrate all aspects of the branch including sales, service, people, and the core operations. A dependable leader is one who places the spotlight on achieving the team's goals and not on his or her personal accomplishment.

In my 17 years playing as an offensive lineman, I lived behind the scenes. I never scored the winning touchdown, caught a pass to win a game, or sacked a quarterback to end the game. Yet my job was still very important--I was to protect the quarterback so that he could throw the winning pass and block for the running back in order that he could score the winning touchdown. Many times the only time I would get individual credit was when things went wrong. However, the success achieved when everyone did his job was much greater than any personal recognition. This is also the thinking of a steadfast leader. The "big picture" is much greater than any one position, and a successful manager will coach his or her staff to recognize this on a daily basis.

Not only is a strong manager selfless, but he or she is also highly influential. Because leadership is influence, it is the branch manager who must promote an environment that welcomes change and transition. Often times, the way in which change is accepted is the way it is presented. A manager who maintains a high level of passion for improvement and progress spreads optimism to his or her employees. This way of thinking also will contribute to other areas like quality teamwork, effective communication, and competent problem solving skills.

Finally, it is within the power of the leader and the team to see that success is reached. In doing so, each team member must be playing in a position where he or she contributes the most to the overall mission of the organization. Each player must continue to grow and develop skills that help improve his or her job performance.

The "big picture" must remain the focus, and all aspects of the branch must be pulled together to work as one unit towards the greater goal. Together the right leader, the right employees, the right attitudes, and the right organization will lead right to success. Vince Lombardi once stated, "Individual commitment to a group effort-that is what makes a team work, a company work, a society work, a civilization work." This, too, is what makes a branch work.

The Key To Happiness

Author Name: Stacie Standifer

Company Name: City Publications (Nashville Lifestyles and Murfreesboro Magazine)

Title: Founder and Publisher

Phone: 615-259-3636

Website: www.southernsophisticate.com

Business Description:
The function of my business is to serve as content director and business development leader for both our print and online publications. Cited as the Magazine of Music City, Nashville Lifestyles is one of the top city magazines in the region and country. I also run a blog tied to the magazine content, titled The Southern Sophisticate.

If there is one thing that I can attribute to my success in business, it would be exactly the same that has been a benefit in every facet of my life. I fully believe that surrounding yourself with honest, talented and creative people is the key to happiness and success.

When I first started the magazines, I had zero experience in the field. What I did have was a passion for the cities as well as a desire to enter an industry I found fascinating. My only true assets were a good sense of my audience and a love of magazines. Otherwise, I entered into the venture completely blind. Because of this, I wasn't held to standards of hiring people with specific experience or skills, but rather, chose others that I was drawn to in some way. That doesn't mean that they didn't have to develop basic skills for the job, but the qualifications were not that important. I wanted to work with people that I liked and was excited to talk to. My best sales reps turned out to be a former schoolteacher, another from the public relations side of the music business and others among non-related fields. My controller today is someone I knew from growing up who had previously worked in real estate. The best office manager/assistant I've ever had came to me from selling mortgage loans. All very random, but great fits just the same.

I respect and treasure relationships, and business is all about relationships. While those on my staff were important to cultivate, I've been equally devoted to those in the city that really have no direct tie to my business. I have learned more from other business owners and entrepreneurs than I ever did in college or the countless conferences and continuing education I've engaged in. But again, I've elected to make friends with those that I like first, knowing that the benefits to the business or to my life will come with those choices.

It is because of the people on my team and my supporters outside of the office that I've been able to make it through good times and bad. The best part? Being around people I truly enjoy has made the entire journey so much more worth it.

Don't Gimme No Lines And Keep Your Hype To Yourself

Author Name: Bob Hutchins

Company Name: Buzzplant

Title: Founder

Phone: 615 550-2305

Email: bob@buzzplant.com

Website: www.Buzzplant.com/

Business Description:
Incorporating cutting-edge technology and creative design, Buzzplant helps companies, individuals, and groups communicate their story via word of mouth by using all forms of technology. That is what sets Buzzplant apart.

Being Authentic in the Recommendation Age

Information Age marketing, if we can be totally honest here, is primarily concerned with managing what consumers believe about a product or service. Even advertising stills like billboards and magazine ads are designed to impress one's imagination more than inform. The public has wised up and assumes that what a brand knows about its products is filtered for advertising. This is less negative than it sounds because everyone accepts the norm of showing one's better side and putting one's best foot forward, etc. Consumers know and accept that hype is part of the game. This arrangement worked pretty well for brands and marketers in the past because they controlled most of the information to which consumers had access.

The Information Age allowed service and product sellers to present their best side and gift-wrap their public exposure with slick advertising. Consumers have been wearied by over a hundred years of information control marketing and almost two generations of mass marketing. To a large extent marketers have earned the distrust that underscores a good bit of public cynicism about big business.

According to consumer opinion research in 2005, 76% percent of American consumers believe companies don't tell the truth in advertising and 60% of consumers surveyed reported having a more negative opinion of marketing and advertising than in years past. A June 2011 report by Nielsen Research may support a slightly gentler perspective of consumer attitudes.

Guidelines for Authenticity in the Recommendation Age

First and foremost, again, is thinking long-term. Grow your market's recognition of your authenticity the way you expect your kid to earn your trust. It generally takes time but there will be valuable opportunities to leap ahead. Set a policy and only change it to more accurately present your company's authentic identity.

Don't project a false image—don't imply your company has a capability that doesn't square with the truth as it is right now. Make sure consumers know who you are, not just who you hope someday to be, and especially not who you merely want consumers to think you are. That may sound like your mother talking but the forced honesty in social media marketing shows how entrenched deceptive habits have become. Brands are now facing the reality that the unvarnished truth comes out very quickly. So a vacation spot that advertises an onsite health club better have a lot more than an exercise class in the parking lot if it wants to be competitive for long.

Don't stonewall, sugar coat, or moderate answers to consumer questions and complaints. A modulated tone and manicured reply to something negative doesn't soften the blow for you or your customer. It's just more manipulation and only ticks people off. Or shall I say, it could be perceived, though unintended, as evasive and concealing, leading to an unprofitable environment of resistance and discontentment. See the difference? Just keep it real and conversational. Show your fun side, not your good side. When we try to show our good side we're thinking about our bad side and are anxious to cover it up. Think of it this way—Social media isn't a conference of perfect, beautiful people. In social media we get together with new friends and old to help each other and have fun.

When you're genuinely having fun it's hard to be false. Go into it expecting to have a good time with people even when you have to deal with problems. Follow along or even participate in the social media streams of other companies like Southwest Airlines and Coca Cola to get in the groove of how they make it enjoyable. Fess up to screw-ups. Do it fast before social media drags it out of you. Nothing will be worse for your authentic brand identity than being outed for covering something up. Bad news doesn't get better with age, so use it to admit what everyone already knows—companies are human institutions and none of them are perfect.

Company officers and employees make mistakes and sometimes act foolishly. Even if a screw-up is really bad, if you deal with it quickly, authentically, and with intent for customer advantage you'll gain from it in the long run. To their credit Microsoft didn't blame shift or downplay the ill-advised tweet about Amy Winehouse. They accepted the guilt, apologized, and in a few weeks the negative buzz died out with minimal lasting impact.

In December of 2011, Federal Express had to deal with the very unpleasant impact of a well-circulated video showing a package, containing a video monitor, being tossed over a customer's fence. Fed Ex wisely responded with emphatic public apologies to the customer and made restitution. Their expression of intolerance for such package handling probably means the deliveryman was immediately looking for another job. Fortunately for Fed Ex, a long-standing reputation for good service has limited the lingering impact of the incident. By answering to the problem quickly and without excuses, it made it a non-issue and likely resulted in a net gain to consumer confidence. Their response also put Fed Ex in the position of looking like a good sport when late night TV spoofs of the incident made fun of them. And, at best, this was also free brand promotion.

Every company makes mistakes. If you're lucky a competitor may even try to kick you when you're down, making you look like the noble underdog. Here's how you respond to that in social media: "It kind of hurt to hear them say that because they're good competitors and we've always admired how they relate to other companies in our industry." Well, maybe that's fudging a little if you don't really admire them but you get the idea. Like I always say—play nice. There's a sly remark in the Bible about putting hot coals on your enemy's head this way!

Keys To Unselfish Communication

Author Name: Pierce Mars

Company Name: Marrs Coaching

Title: Sales and Communication Coach, Speaker and Podcaster.

Phone: 615.59.COACH

Email: pierce@marrscoaching.com

Website: http://www.marrscoaching.com/

Business Description:

We provide "relationship sales" and effective communication training to businesses, sales teams and entrepreneurs. We specialize in an "individual" approach helping clients maximize their personality, skills and abilities.

"The less people know, the more they yell."—*Seth Godin*

Developing effective communication skills is imperative to success in all areas of your life. These skills can improve your ability to understand a person or situation, enable you to resolve differences, build trust and rapport, and create an environment where problem solving and win-win solutions are possible. The concept is simple but the execution can be difficult, unless we dedicate ourselves to learning a few basic principles.

The first question we must ask--Is it more effective to communicate with others as you would have them communicate with you, or should we communicate with others in the manner they prefer to be communicated with?

Most everyone would agree to the latter, however, it is not what most people do. Stephen R. Covey stated in his bestselling book 7 Habits of Highly Effective People that most people listen with the intent to reply, not to understand.

If you want to communicate effectively, you must take an unselfish approach. I teach people that in a successful sales process, you must remember that it is never about you--It is always about the other person. By understanding this one principle, you can better connect with your business associates as well as your spouse, children and friends.

The following are three keys to help you become an unselfish, effective communicator:

Active Listening

"The most basic of all human needs is the need to understand and be understood. The best way to understand people is to listen to them." ~ Ralph Nichols

Most people believe they are good listeners. In fact, most people are not! Listening can be the most effective form of communication but it is possibly the most difficult to master. Research suggests that we remember between twenty-five and fifty percent of what we hear.

Active listening goes beyond merely listening to the words being spoken but, more importantly, understanding the complete message behind those words.

One mistake I see people make repeatedly is assuming they know the answer or solution before the other person has completed a thought. This is very offensive to the person speaking and can undermine your ability to connect with them. Let them complete their thought and ask good questions to confirm you have a good understanding of what they are saying. Quickly offering a solution before they have finished their thought will not make you look smarter. It will make you seem rude and they will feel agitated in the process.

The first step to becoming a good listener is a genuine concern for what the other person is saying. Developing this skill is difficult, however, when mastered it will put you on the road to being a successful communicator.

Non-verbal Communication

"What you do speaks so loud that I cannot hear what you say." ~ Ralph Waldo Emerson

Studies have shown that fifty-five percent of communication is non-verbal, with your tone of voice and the words you are using coming in at thirty-eight percent and seven percent respectively. Regardless of where you weigh in on the percentages, to communicate effectively, this subject cannot be ignored.

The way you listen, look, move, and react tells the other person whether or not you care, if you're being truthful, and how well you're listening. When your body language lines up with your tone of voice and the words you are saying, you become a powerful communicator. The other person will feel heard and this will increase trust and rapport.

If these characteristics do not line up, they generate confusion, tension and mistrust. Can you recall a time when you were speaking to someone and they were distracted by other people during a lunch meeting or continually looking at their smart phones? How did it make you feel?

Better communication requires you to be sensitive to body language and the non-verbal cues you are sending, as well as noticing those cues in the other person. By learning to recognize these cues, you will be in tune with the thoughts and feelings of others.

Here are some ways you can improve your non-verbal communication: Be conscious of your facial expressions, use good posture, make good eye contact, offer a firm handshake and respect the personal space of others. One more thing, leave your phone in your pocket!

When you talk . . .

"The royal road to a person's heart is to talk to him about the things he treasures most." ~ Dale Carnegie

Dale Carnegie dedicated a section of his best selling book, How To Win Friends and Influence People, to the art of how to make people like you. Of the six ways Carnegie mentions, rule number five deals with talking in terms of the other person's interest.

We cannot achieve this if we have no idea what the other person truly values or is really interested in. I believe in the 30/70 rule. We should speak thirty percent of the time, leaving the other person seventy percent of the time to express themselves.

Let's be honest. Most people are naturally self-interested. We always look for ourselves in a photo, and we love to share the exciting things going on in our life. Humbling yourself and allowing other people to speak their mind will draw people to you and increase your influence.

Summary

Unselfish communication begins with understanding that people respond positively to being heard and understood. It is human nature to talk in terms of our own interests. That being said, in order to build trust and rapport we must set our agenda aside and focus on the other person.

Developing the art of unselfish communication will help you easily connect with anyone, motivate people, resolve conflicts and draw people to you. It will also help you strengthen personal and business relationships by thoroughly understanding the needs of others.

Building Meaningful
Business Relationships
Nashville-style

Author Name: Terry Humphrey

Company Name: Terry Humphrey LLC

Title: Principal

Phone: 615-326-1341

Website: www.terryhumphreyllc.com

Business Description:
Business and Personal Coaching—I help small businesses create and execute their plans for success. I help individuals reduce the overwhelming task of doing it all and help them 'get out of their own way' to achieve their vision and goals.

Terry Humphrey, Business & Executive Coach, is a local expert on the art and science of effective networking and building business relationships. Terry has lived and worked in Middle Tennessee for 25 years. Her expertise is helping her clients create and execute their plans and get out of their own way through building self-awareness and the ability to sell themselves. An avid cyclist, Terry is also devoted to wellness as a practice of successful business owners.

"The quality of your life is the quality of your relationships."—*Tony Robbins*

One thing that I know for sure is that Nashville is a relationship town, or more accurately a "connection" town. Being an influential city in the Volunteer State, Nashville is known for its uniquely nice residents and for a history of people who are truly connected in meaningful ways in the business community. Seriously— people here blow the horn of their car to let you into a turn lane, not to demonstrate frustration. And that's one of many idiosyncrasies that make Nashville such an easy place to build family, friends and a wonderful way of life.

Besides being a uniquely nice place to visit and a great town to live in, Nashville is known for building business through relationships, as opposed to selling solutions just on merit. Business owners want to know you, not just know your products. They want to trust and believe in you. The good news about building long-term relationships is longer-term success for you and your business. The drawback is that relationship-building takes longer and in today's fast-paced business world, it sometimes feels like progress with relationship-building takes too much time and effort.

If you've ever dated anyone, have a spouse or significant other or have friends, you know that relationships are complex, even in a nice place like Nashville. It's a bit of a dance, discovering what the other person's likes and dislikes are, what he or she does or doesn't believe in and figuring out what their concerns and pressures are that create an opportunity to connect. There is also a real need to develop a level of consistency and persistence that makes you trustworthy. People in Nashville expect proof, and if you are introduced to them through a trusted friend and advisor, then that's much better proof than any report you can produce.

Nashville is a big, small town. So everyone seems to know someone that you know, and often no one is separated by more than two, as opposed to the conventional belief that we are all related by six degrees of separation. Relationships are not only with clients or prospective clients, but also with friends, acquaintances, vendors, employees, and even with your competitors.

To build better relationships, there are a few things that you should master:

Know your communication style and personal brand

Knowing who you are and if your personal brand is consistent with whom you are is a critical success factor for building relationships. How you communicate, how you handle conflict, how you come across in conversation and the way that you present yourself in image—tone and energy—all send a strong message about who you are to your clients and prospects. Sometimes it helps to have a friend, mentor or coach hold up a mirror that helps you see yourself as others see you. Perception **IS** reality, particularly with first impressions, and a perception, right or wrong, often sets the tone for building a relationship. I use a variety of assessment tools and questioning with my clients to help build a better understanding of not only how they communicate, but also how others perceive their communication style as a tool to improve relationship-building skills.

Improve your ability to really listen actively to the other person

Active listening is an important skill in business, whether you are building a relationship or leading a team. Do you plan what you are going to say while a client or prospect is speaking? You can miss important cues in the conversation and important changes in body language and many other indicators will help you understand the other person and their needs and desires much better. Others can tell when you are tuned into what they are saying versus what you are planning to say. The ability to figure out what would help a client or prospect achieve their goals is an art and a science that really characterizes long-term business relationships.

Know how you define and demonstrate integrity

Integrity in business often translates to being trustworthy and honest behavior and communicates. Integrity generally means that you are consistently who you appear to be and that what you stand for is obvious to those who do business with you. One skill that will help you build more trust and demonstrate integrity is to develop the ability to ask clarifying questions to insure that you understand the expectations of the other person. The more you clarify your understanding, the more they will feel heard and the more accurate you will be in following up. This skill also supports you being worthy of trust since your follow-through will be more accurately delivered.

Create a system that will allow you to follow up consistently and in a way that is meaningful to the other person

Follow up, or how to stay in touch with people and not let details fall through the cracks, is consistently an area where my clients ask for help. Creating a system and process for following up on your promises is another critical success factor for building strong, long-term relationships. And having integrity in what you do makes it necessary that you have a system to follow up with people and track activities. I think about this skill as the one that really sets someone apart in a relationship. If you always follow through on the promises that you make, no matter how small, your relationships will flourish. Knowing when and what to promise, then having a system to make sure that you follow through on your commitment will serve you not only in building relationships, but also in all aspects of your business or career.

Build a community of people for your business and your clients

The purpose of building relationships does not have to be just about increasing sales. For example, if you are an entrepreneur or small business owner, your networking and relationship-building may also help you develop a list of advisors for your business and your clients. Perhaps you need to build a relationship with an attorney or a CPA who could not only be a referral source, but could also help you in your business and help clients in their businesses. Building relationships with a wide variety of experts in Middle Tennessee will help you become more well-rounded in business and lead to opportunities that you might not have considered without these varied insights and experiences. Through meaningful connections with people over time, you and your business will flourish.

As a Nashpreneur, building strong relationships over time is a "must have" skill in order for you and your business to grow. Because of the generous nature of the people of Nashville, you'll find opportunity to seek and find the support you need to build successful relationships.

Love What You Do

Name: David W. Adams, CPA, CFP®

Company: Southwestern Investment Group/Raymond James Financial Services, Inc.

Title: Vice-President

Phone: 615-861-1621

Website: www.davidadamsfinancialplanning.com

Business Description: David and his team provide clients with comprehensive wealth management to include retirement, estate, investment, and tax planning. Over the years their team has specialized in helping retirees, corporate executives, athletes, and musicians manage and preserve their assets. As Vice-President of Southwestern Investment Group, David has helped the firm become the top-producing branch of Raymond James Financial Services, Inc., who recently inducted David as a member of its 2012 Chairman's Council, consisting of the top 1% of the firm's advisors in the country

As I sit here and reflect on the last 12 years building the Wealth Management practice I have today, several key thoughts and lessons learned come to my mind. First, I would venture to say, passion for helping others and enjoying what you do is the key recipe for success in any business. I started my career in a profession without these ingredients, but it led me down a path to find my place of passion. I spend every day meeting with and trying to help people, all while loving what I do and earning a living. You can't replace these ingredients with anything else and I'll stand firm in saying this is the most important aspect of building any business. Finding fulfillment in your daily work helps build a solid foundation.

Another key lesson learned has been hiring the right people and positioning myself with the best team. Early in my career I naively thought that I had to do everything and touch everything that went out the door. I couldn't have been more wrong. The best years of the practice occurred when I invested more in my team and entrusted them, releasing some control I had held on to for too long. I am now able to focus on the most important client issues and critical aspects of the practice while allowing my staff to grow and accept more challenges. It's a win/win/win—the staff gets more confidence and growth in their careers, my time is freed up for new things and the client gets unmatched service from the entire team. Why didn't I think of this the first few years???

While there are many more insightful lessons I could share and wisdom one could obtain from others in the community who have been doing this for far longer than I, I'll conclude with this: Surround yourself with people smarter and wiser than you. Once again, looking back I see that early in building my business I thought I had all the answers. I didn't. Some of the most profound growth for me professionally and personally came from finding mentors that could coach me. I became a sponge for good advice built from years of failures that turned into great life lessons. We can't do this alone-- as humans we need relationships, others (and God) to help us when we fail or become scared and to help us avoid big, fundamental mistakes.

At the end of the day, we need each other, our faith and community to grow and maintain a successful business. We are blessed to live in an amazing city with unselfish people willing to help, and what a great opportunity we all have in front of us. Love what you do, surround yourself with a great team and lean on others during times of need, allowing them to help you to simply grow as a person. We all win when we operate this way.

720 Cool Springs Blvd., Suite 100, Franklin, TN 37067

Securities offered through Raymond James Financial Services, Inc. Member FINRA/SIPC Any opinions are those of David W. Adams and not necessarily those of RJFS or Raymond James

Investment Rules For Entrepreneurs

Author Name: Will T. Tenpenny

Company Name: Edward Jones Investments

Title: Financial Advisor

Phone: 615-302-4598

Website: www.EdwardJones.com/Willtenpenny

Business Description:
Our Mission is to provide the investments, services, and information individuals need to achieve their financial goals by taking a personal interest in our clients' lives.

As a Financial Advisor with Edward Jones, I have worked with many companies and learned a great deal from my experiences. I have seen great ideas fail and bad ideas thrive. There are many things that we as business owners need to learn and do for our companies but here are 5 investment rules to begin the process:

Rule 1 - Build a successful TEAM

Many people invent great ideas, think up great concepts or have a great product, BUT in the end, their success is only as good as the team around them. When beginning a business, an owner needs to have three best friends to get started. As our country grows, it is very tough to build a business and also stay current on laws outside of your focus. It is important to know enough information to be dangerous but also make sure you hire three best friends. As a new entrepreneur, you must have a great CPA, financial advisor, and a lawyer. By having these three teammates you get off on the right foot. Any good idea or business will fall short of its potential if it does not follow proper tax laws, business laws and have proper financials to run the company. So building the right team is key.

After you have recruited your three first members, depending on what kind of business you do, your next step is hiring quality employees. So often people hire someone to just do the job. You do not get them to "buy" into your plan and your vision. It is crucial to have your staff on board with you because they are the face of your company. As an owner, you must allow these team members to share in your success and your failures because that will create a healthy business environment.

Rule 2- Focus on what you can CONTROL

As a type-A personality, I want to control everything but unfortunately controlling everything is impossible. I have realized over the years the most successful business owners put quality people around them so they only have to oversee what they are doing instead of doing everything themselves. This allows the owner to focus on what they can control. You cannot control who buys, what people say or how people will react. What you can control is how many people you present your product or company to, how you dictate your message of your product or company and how you represent yourself. If I have learned one thing being in business it is this--you cannot control who will or won't buy but you can control how many people you talk to. It is a numbers game, so control the numbers you can control.

Rule 3- Build an EMERGENCY FUND

Now most of you might be thinking, "Ok this is the first bit of investment advice this guy has given me yet." I believe the first two rules are very important and are part of the business planning, but rule three is where the rubber meets the road. Business owners have to deal with cash flow issues. There are good and bad times and when the bad times come (not if) the entrepreneurs that are prepared will be those who keep their doors open. People always ask me, "Well, I how much do I need?". There is no perfect answer because it depends on many factors. When I was 18 years old, I owned a company called, Tenpenny's Lawn Care LLC. I had owned it for several years and it was a small company, but it began to rapidly grow. I eventually bought a new truck, mowers, and other equipment. I felt like I was invincible because the money was rolling in and I was growing rapidly and investing it wisely back into my business for future growth. Well after I went through this massive growth phase, I had several things go wrong all at once. I had a mower spindle blow out, a weed eater break, a transmission go out in my truck, and if that wasn't enough, I had a client skip town owing me $3,200. No one can prepare for everything, but you can prepare. At that moment I called my Dad and asked him, "Why do bad things only seem to happen to poor people trying to build a future?". His words of wisdom still ring loud and clear in my head. He said, "Son, bad things happen to everyone but rich people can afford it because they prepare for it." So proper emergency funds are vital to the success of an individual's finances but also for a company.

Rule 4- Create a BUSINESS RETIREMENT PLAN

When I speak to small business owners about their game plan for retirement, I get one of two reactions. The first one sometimes is a deer-in-the-headlights look. Eyes get wide, gloss over and the next few words are usually . . . "um, ah, well" or just silence. The second reaction is a quick statement, "My business is my retirement." I agree that the single best asset for an entrepreneur is their business, but what happens if business gets bad? When times are tough you cannot walk outside, chip a brick off your building and eat it. You never know what your company will be worth when it comes time to sell. Plus there are so many tax advantages to setting up business retirement accounts. I am not a tax professional so set up a time to sit down with your financial advisor and CPA because it can really benefit you and your company. Each company's needs are different, but owners miss major opportunities in this area every year.

Rule 5- Understand RISK

Risk is a four-letter word we are all used to hearing. It is something we as entrepreneurs love yet hate. Cash, stocks, bonds, mutual funds, and real estate . . . everything has risk. Knowing how to manage risk is very important in our businesses and our financial planning. As business owners, it is what makes us take the leap of faith into our own companies. We believe owning a company is better than a nine-to-five job. Entrepreneurs would not make the money they make if it was easy. If it was in fact easy, then everyone would be doing it. So set goals, define needs, understand risk, and allow time to do the rest.

These rules helped me build my business and several other business owners I have worked with. I hope these 5 rules can be the building blocks to your success as a entrepreneur.

Be Specific When Asking For What You Need

Author Name: Tim Cummings

Company Name: Cummings Enterprises

Title: CEO & President

Phone: 615-945-2899

Website: http://www.ybuf.com/

Business Description:
I guide business owners step-by-step, through the process of growing their business and assembling an appropriate board of advisors. I use my extensive experience in engineering, as well as managing small, large, and family businesses to help business-owners achieve their vision for their company. In addition to a strong planning and sequencing approach to business, I have a special gifting in the area of utilizing technology to build client relationships. I am particularly attracted to business owners seeking to live out their faith in their business.

As I work daily to help entrepreneurs speak out their vision for their business and then execute that vision in proper sequence, I have learned a truth that greatly increases a business person's probability for success. That truth is to be specific when stating your needs.

Successful business people know that one key to their success is networking. Through networking we expand the reach of our businesses, locate resources from which we can draw, and develop relationships that can be leveraged to achieve greater success. Even though we are armed with this understanding, when we enter a room of associates, we often act from a sense of scarcity. Despite our needs, as we look around the room, our core assumption is that no one in the space really has exactly what we need. At this point, as we verbalize our request, we tend to become very general in that request. "If I am just broad enough in my question, maybe someone will suggest something that might work!" And the results are usually miserable! Let's consider why this is.

We all want to be successful. When we invest time and effort to help someone else, we really want to give them what they need. If someone is vague in their "ask", then they will not be sure what it takes to be successful. More often than not, they will tell the person that they will try to help them get what they need, but not really do anything more.

Consider what happens when I choose to be specific in my request. Let's just assume I walked into a group and said I was looking for a red-headed step-child. This request is both specific and visual. The first possible response may be, "I've got one of those. How can I help?". . . . But what else could be a likely response?

How about, "I don't have a red-headed step-child. How about a blonde one? Will that work?" This response would probably be followed by someone else in the room saying, "I color hair. I could make the blonde a red head!" So now we are developing alternatives. Someone else might chime in, "I don't have a step-child, but I do have a red headed nephew/niece. Would that work?" This is an alternative developing a parallel track—something that expands the pool of available resources.

Then of course, other responses could focus on where appropriate children could be located. i.e. "Have you looked at a day care? Looked at a swimming pool?

Looked at Chucky Cheese?" Now we are developing alternative sources to find that for which I am looking.

See how much more productive my specific request has become to the task at hand? There is another benefit to a precise request. Our minds are protected by a mental wall that shields us from many, if not most, possible thoughts. This shield allows us to focus on tasks at hand. It lets us ignore "noise" that occurs all around us. There is a secret to this mental wall—it can be penetrated by the right key words. When I am specific in my petition, I encode key words in your mental wall. Over the next several days, as you are out and about, you will find yourself noticing all sorts of red-headed step children. It is not that suddenly you are surrounded by them, but that by my arming you with the specific item asked for, it becomes a key word which allows you to notice, despite your protective wall. You will soon be on the phone to let me know where you are finding all of these red headed step-children.

To recap, we often enter into networking opportunities with a scarcity mindset. We assume that no one has what we need and therefore become very general in our requests. To improve the rate of success in getting that for which you ask, be specific. You will be amazed at the number of successes you will score in a very short period of time. One final comment--when you ask someone to help you locate a specific request, make sure they know how to get in touch with you to report back what they discover. This tip will revolutionize your networking and will accelerate your business growth and success.

The Business Of Radio

Author Name: Phil Valentine

Website: www.PhilValentine.com

Email: Phil@PhilValentine.com

Business Description:
Author of the book, The Conservative's Handbook and host of the
Phil Valentine show.

The radio business is one of those rare businesses in which our customers are not our clients. Let me explain. Most businesses produce a product or service then market that product or service to a targeted customer base. In radio, we target a listener base but they are not the ones paying the bill, at least not directly. The advertisers are the ones paying the bills and they, in some cases, are not our listeners.

Agency business, for example, is purchased on behalf of advertising clients who buy all over the country. They may never even hear the show but buy on numbers. Local sales are made to clients who, in all likelihood, are familiar with the show but, again, are not necessarily the customer. So, it's an interesting line we walk between pleasing the customer (the listener) and pleasing the client (the advertiser).

There has been a conventional wisdom in the talk radio business that "talk is talk", meaning they believe talk radio listeners will tolerate many more commercials than a music radio listener. I would ask the same proponents of that philosophy if they would mind loading up the music station with jingles since music is music. Of course, the answer is no.

Talk radio is really no different than any other radio format. It has to keep the listener's interest. You don't do that by running them off with excessive commercials. You "play the hits" just like a music station in that you provide stimulating, informative and entertaining talk on the hot issues of the day. If it's a really hot issue, like a really hot song, you "play" it more often.

But our show and our network, Cumulus Media Networks (formerly the ABC Radio Network) are taking a trend-setting approach to The Phil Valentine Show. While most syndicated talk shows are breaking for four or five minutes at the :15 and :45 breaks, we break for only two minutes. With many of our affiliates a minute of that break is traffic, a service they want and need and are waiting to hear. That means in many cases, those twice-per-hour breaks only contain a minute of commercials. I believe this is going to revolutionize the talk radio product.

Research shows that many people either tune out or turn down during breaks. The reason being they find it difficult to endure a five-minute bombardment of commercials. But two minutes is doable for even the biggest critic of commercial breaks.

So how on earth does one make money by cutting the spot load in a talk radio hour? It's very similar to how the government brings in more money when it cuts income taxes. Each time the federal government has cut the income tax rate the income to the government has gone up. The premise is simple. You cut taxes, which stimulates growth in the private sector, which creates more income, thus creating more income tax.

The same principle applies in radio.

Radio share is a product of two things: cume and time-spent-listening (TSL). Cume is the term used for the raw number of listeners at any given time. TSL is how long each listener stays tuned to your station. The share, which is what the advertisers look at when determining how much they'll pay, is a formula based on TSL and cume. If you can hold listeners through a break your TSL goes up. And if you gain the reputation of a show with fewer commercials your cume goes up.

At that point it becomes a simple issue of supply and demand. Radio shows set their advertising rates based on share so it makes sense that if your share goes up you can charge more for each commercial.

I had one listener complain that I was driving up the price of commercials on my show, thus driving up the price of the products advertised. He obviously doesn't understand economics. Advertising generally doesn't drive up the price. In fact, it helps to bring down the cost. It's all about volume. No advertiser is going to spend more on advertising than it creates in new business. It's a lot cheaper per burger for McDonald's to make a million burgers on any given day rather than just a thousand. It's the volume of new and repeat business that keeps companies advertising. Otherwise they would never do it.

As for the shorter spot breaks, they also benefit the advertiser in that a) more people are hearing the message and b) that message doesn't get lost in a long spot break. It really is a revolutionary concept and one that I believe will drive talk radio for decades to come.

But the challenge will always be juggling the customer with the client. If you make the customer (the listener) happy, there will always be clients lined up to advertise. After all, the customer is always right.

If You Are Not On The Edge, You Are Taking Up Too Much Space

Author Name: Mike Cotter

Company Name:
Yeoman's in the Fork Rare Book & Document Gallery

Title: Director of Operations

Phone: 615-983-6460

Website: www.yeomansinthefork.com

Business Description:
We are proud purveyors of rare books and documents. We consistently strive to harness the technology of today to sell pieces of the past.

My name is Mike Cotter and I am a rare bookman. Alongside my trusted friends, partners and financial backers, we opened Yeoman's in the Fork Rare Books to the public in 2009. I opened my first rare bookselling outlet nearly seven years ago. I am a functional bibliophile and I have a passion for sharing my love for collecting books with anyone who will listen. With the help of several forward-thinking tech guys that I have hired over the years, we can now spread the collecting message with hundreds and thousands via the internet, Facebook, Twitter etc. At this point we offset our amazing in-person platform with the virtual world. You see I am old-school when it comes to marketing. I believe the old methods of print ads, physical trade show appearances and in-person classes on collecting and the like in our open shop are the most important part of my business as it provides me with direct contact with my potential clients.

Continuing to think that this is paramount is ok, but you had better be thinking about how you are going to get out there (virtually speaking of course) or you are going to have to hang out the 'Going Out of Business Sale' sign faster than you think. Our virtual presence shores up the gaps and gets clients in the door. The 'meat' is inevitably the most important part of our rare bookstore, but getting our message viral has and will continue to be the link between the 'meat' and money in the door.

Folks ask me all the time what it is like to be a rare bookseller in a digital age and I sometimes have to laugh to myself. One of the integral pieces that make a book both sought after as well as valuable is scarcity. If we are truly living in a digital age and if print books are in the slow fade, it stands to reason that collectors are going to find it harder and harder to get copies of the books that have meant something to them in their lives. Scarcity already exists and we are just enhancing the perception that books are becoming more and more scarce quite frankly. Sounds pretty good me.

While there is no direct road map to success and everyone puts their own spin on it, I have personally relied upon one major maxim in my life that gets me started and keeps me motivated. "**If you are not on the edge, you are taking up too much space**." I have pushed the envelope in my life. I have seen past boundaries that might cause others to turn and run for the hills just south of the Harpeth River. You must keep a level head, but continue to push through the financial and mental struggles for what you believe to be your destiny is all-important in my opinion. Recognize and understand that there are going to be hard times. There are going to be sleepless nights. You are going to miss out on an amazing deal on a first edition book every now and then. Books that come your way are going to become valuable and you will have let them go thinking they were just a fad. If it were easy, everyone would be doing it. Learn from your mistakes, but do what makes you happy and you are going to be satisfied with the outcome (whatever it may be) as you have lived by your passions.

If you are like me and you are doing business in Nashville and her surrounding areas, you will soon recognize that she has many ways of aiding in your daily business life. At Yeoman's, we share our knowledge of rare books and middle Tennessee with many visitors. We have come to rely upon our thick southern accents and our staunch view that anything fried is always better. We believe in biscuits, cornbread and the power of the gothic southern writer. This area is steeped in tradition and we are covered in a southern tradition that is thicker than kudzu, which can be used to our advantage anytime we are out and about while supporting our business. Is it a feather in our hat to be thought of as Southern? While I can't answer that, I can state that being from the South and sharing some of my uniquely southern experiences has most certainly gotten me a call back. I CAN say that I work tirelessly to continue the traditions of the southern gentleman and our business culture reflects the fact that we work and speak from the heart. We are here to make a profit, but we are also here to genuinely aid in your book-buying and/or collecting endeavors. We offer a relationship and our word is thicker than any contract could ever be. Yeoman's in the Fork Rare Books does Antiquarian Book Fairs from coast to coast and we represent the South as best we can. We are a living example that folks do generally relate to you if you are genuine, and being uniquely southern and genuine is just a bonus when it comes to name and brand recognition.

Keep up the hard work Nashville! This is the land of opportunity and if we can make a go of a rare bookstore in the middle of the hills of Tennessee, then I am afraid I have left you with no further excuses. Good luck and be sure to drop by our shop in Leiper's Fork, TN for a visit and a glass of iced tea. We have a front porch swing waiting for ya . . .

Where Do Dreams Go To Die—Or Do They?

Author Name: Dan Miller

Company Name: 48 Days LLC

Title: Director of Opportunities

Phone: 615-595-8872

Website: www.48Days.com

Business Description:
Our mission at 48 Days is to foster the process of imagining, dreaming and introspection to help people find their calling and true path, and to translate that into meaningful, purposeful and profitable daily work.

As an author and business coach I hear lots of questions from people who would like to have their own business—but talk themselves out of it without even trying.

Here's an example:

"Dan, I am an introvert who is not good at selling. However, I would really love to have my own business. Should I give up this dream?

First, let's look at "Should I give up this dream?" What happens to a dream when you give up on it? Where does it go? I have a feeling it takes up residence in a section of our mind and spirit and starts to cause problems. What if it's those discarded dreams that are throwing obstacles in our path? What if that low self-confidence is coming from a buried dream seeking expression? What if the frustration you're feeling at your job is really coming from the unsettled feeling of a dream that's being neglected?

How many people do you know who at 43 have discovered they're living out someone else's dream or expectations rather than being authentic to their own? I suspect it's like having a discarded piece of cheese in the back of your refrigerator. You can ignore it but it will start to change form, to mold, to grow its own little community of fungus and to emanate a smell that screams for attention. I think our dreams stick around until they get attention as well. And with the undercurrent of smothered dreams you will find it difficult to release your best talents in any other way. You cannot do something well that does not engage your strongest passions and dreams.

In working with mid-life career changers, I find the best options are found not by superimposing the latest trends or hottest current business ideas, but by peeling away the layers of life that have clouded their childhood dreams. And it's by taking a fresh look at those recurring themes that are begging for attention that we find the choices that are likely to result in meaningful, fulfilling and profitable ventures. Yes, we can scrape the mold off the cheese and find that there is still life, vitality, and the seed of new life just waiting to be released.

I don't think we can casually just give up on a dream or tell it to go away.

You may not act on it but I'm quite confident that the dream is still gasping for breath as you try to keep it hidden. Look around you—you can see plenty of others who show the evidence of buried dreams in headaches, back pain, persistent cough and other more serious health maladies. Is the homeless guy down on 2nd Avenue really unable to provide his own way or is he suffering the backlash of buried dreams?

And here's the other part of the question: So you're an introvert who's not good at selling. Why are you not good at selling? Selling skills are not something you're born with any more than are the skills to do brain surgery. We learn how to do both. And you don't have to be an extrovert to learn how to sell any more than you have to be tall to be a surgeon.

If you know you're an introvert, then you'll want to learn selling skills than embrace that. You don't have to change who you are, but you do have to learn to sell the way introverts sell. Create systems and methods for selling where you never have to have nose-to-nose or belly-to-belly interaction with your customers. Look at my business—**48 Days**—In the time I've taken to write these few paragraphs, a whole lot of people have come into **my store**, browsed around, purchased products, signed up for live events and requested coaching. Have I talked to them? No, I'm busy writing this piece. But I have systems in place that allow them to shop in pleasure.

Yes, I do things to invite them in, like writing this article. Like doing the weekly <u>48 Days Podcast</u>, commenting on other people's blogs, writing articles for magazines, providing tons of <u>free resources</u> for anyone looking for meaningful work--but none of those require me to be an extrovert. Just for the record, I too, am an introvert—any inventory you give me will confirm that.

Many million dollar selling systems and businesses are constructed by introverts—extraverts are too busy talking and having a good time to pay attention to the critical details.

You can remain an introvert, learn how to sell effectively and knock it out of the park in your own business. And experience the joy of being authentic and fully alive. And as for that dream, don't think you can walk away from it and from the financial and personal success for which that may be your only possible vehicle. Be authentic to who you are—AND follow your dream and walk into the most exciting chapter of your life.

Getting It All Done: From Strategy Into Action

Author Name: Joanne Eckton

Company Name: Life Choice Expert

Title: Business Performance Architect

Phone: 615-412-9462

Website: http://lifechoiceexpert.com

Business Description:
Joanne Eckton is a Business Performance Architect, helping business owners design their business so that the right people are in the right jobs and the work flows through the organization smoothly and consistently. She is the author of Make Your Job Great: How to Step Up, Own Your Space and Get Your Boss off Your Back. Get a complimentary chapter at http://makeyourjobgreat.com.

I wish . . .

Someday, I'll . . .

I'd like to . . .

If only I . . .

How many times do you hear someone say these words? People tend to wish their lives away, waiting for the magical day when their dreams will come true.

A marketing executive once described the role of her team as taking the customer from, "I want" to "I have". We've all gotten really good at defining what we want, and sometimes even what we don't want. Where we fall short is putting those thoughts into action. Often we feel overwhelmed that the dreams we wish for are unattainable or just too big for us. That may be true at the moment, but it does not need to stay that way. We are all capable of learning, growing and achieving great things. But like the saying goes, "A journey of a thousand miles began with a single step." [1904 Sayings of Lao Tzu] The key to success is taking steps toward your goals with purpose and consistency.

Once you've defined the vision of where you want to take your business in the next 3-5 years, you should define the steps to get there. Your vision is a lofty goal in the clouds, and you need to build a ladder from the ground you are standing on today toward the goal of where you want to be.

4 Steps to DONE

Our "4 Steps to DONE" process is designed to give you a framework for getting things done. Follow these four steps and take your strategy to implementation. DONE stands for Description, Options, Next Steps and Examination. We'll explore each one in detail.

"D" is for Description

The critical first step is to be very clear on what you want to achieve in specific detail and to share that description with others that will help you get there. What will your business look like in a year? In five years? Who are the customers you serve and why is it important to you to do this? Build a vision that has the power to engage you emotionally. You may have financial goals, but you have a reason why those financial goals are important. Understand what those reasons are and they will help you continue to move forward when you inevitably hit problems along the way.

Share this with your team. In a crowd-sourced survey we performed online, the number one factor that employees wanted in their jobs was "a vision we can believe in". Too often those in charge of a company have a great vision, but it is not clearly communicated to the rest of the team. Even if you are a solopreneur, it is important that you share your vision with those who will support you in your business aspirations.

"O" is for Options

List all the options you have for moving toward your goals. What projects can you implement? Do you need to align with a strategic partner? Raise capital? Brainstorm your list of options first without censure. Once you have this list, go back and prioritize them. Look at how well each option fits with your strategic plan, your ability to execute, and the resources you have available.

You have a fixed set of resources. You only have so much money, so much time, and so many people to help you. Make sure all of these resources are aligned on the same priorities. You'll have much more success in achieving your goals when everyone is pulling together and not competing with each other for the same resources. The only competition you should foster is external, not internal.

"N" is for Next Steps

Align action to your priorities. Once you've determined the project you will work on, create a plan. List the tasks that need to get done along with the resources needed for each task. Put a timeline against it. We all tend to procrastinate. The further away the deadline is, the longer we will wait to get started. Build out short-term plans with milestones to keep focused on consistent, immediate action. A proven system for results is to set monthly and weekly goals with tasks listed for each day. Find a rhythm that works for you and your organization, but make sure you break the big goals down into smaller ones to avoid the disappointment of insufficient progress brought about by our natural tendency to procrastinate.

We only have so much mental capacity to create. Wherever possible, build repeatable systems into your business so that these activities are performed the same way every time, regardless of who is doing them. This builds consistency into your results while at the same time eliminating the need to use our creative capacity on a repeatable process. Save that creative thinking for those activities where it is truly necessary.

"E" is for Examination

At each milestone examine where you are. Look at the progress you've made in comparison to the goal. Look at any obstacles that have slowed you down, or risks that you see as a potential obstacle in the future. Be sure to also reassess the overall goal and whether it is still important to your business. Be aware of market changes. Once you've examined these factors, readjust your plans if necessary. You may not always make the interim targets you set for yourself, but it is important to assess whether you are moving in the right direction and make whatever adjustments are needed. Remember a pilot does not fly a plane in a straight line. Rather the pilot must continually make course corrections based on the feedback provided by the instruments on the flight panel. Keep your eyes on your flight panel and adjust your direction as needed.

So the moment you hear another, "I wish", ask the question, "What are you going to do about it?" It will make all the difference in moving dreams towards reality.

Epilogue

How To Get More From David Dutton

Excited about the possibilities of growing your business and want more? If you are looking for better and profitable ways to grow your business, David would like to help you.

If you would like to learn more about how David and his team can help you or your company to become more profitable and have more fun, visit www.Nashpreneur.com where you will find information about:

- *The Ultimate Nashville Marketing Guide*: This free fifty-four minute audio program contains proven marketing methods that you can swipe and deploy right away. It's perfect for the Nashpreneur who wants a boost in their business. It is shipped right to your house. Go to www.Nashpreneur.com/guide
- *Nashpreneur Monthly Marketing Meetup*: A monthly marketing meetup where you get to network with other Nashpreneurs as well as listen in while Dave teaches what's working right now in business. Go to www.Nashpreneur.com/events
- *Nashpreneur Newsletter*: A weekly free newsletter that gives away tips and techniques on building a successful business.
- *St. Judes Strategy Session*: A game changing thirty minute strategy session with David. David gives you 3-4 action steps to take in your business right away. Each session raises money for St. Judes Children's Hospital. For more details visit www.Nashpreneur.com/stjude

David Dutton Live! Discover how you can arrange for David to speak at your meeting, convention, or event. Visit www.Nashpreneur.com today.

Consumer's Guide To Selecting A Professional Online Marketing Consultant For Your Nashville Business

Presented as an Educational Service by
David Dutton, founder
Nashpreneur.com

Read this guide and you'll discover knowledge is power . . .

- **How to avoid four online marketing rip-offs!**
- **Discover six costly misconceptions about online marketing**
- **Eight costly mistakes to avoid when choosing a online marketing consultant**
- **Discover the importance of value, service, and price**
- **Do you want a professional, customer converting website?**
- **The Nashpreneur 100% no-risk guarantee**
- **Discover four steps to a professional, customer converting website**

Hi

My name is David Dutton. I am author of the book, The Ultimate Nashville Business Guide and founder of Nashpreneur.com.

Thank you for calling my consumers awareness hotline. I have been generating new customers and clients using the internet since 2002. In that time, I have found that there are many misconceptions when business professionals hire an online marketing consultant or website designer. So many misconceptions that I decided to create this consumer guide.

I created this guide to help you better understand online marketing. Now, with this information,

you can make an informed, intelligent decision. You'll discover how to avoid website design rip-offs, eight mistakes to avoid when choosing a designer or consultant, and four steps to a powerful, and profitable online presence.

And if you have any questions about online marketing for your Nashville business, you're invited to call me at (615) 796-0104. I have dedicated my business to educating consumers. We'll be happy to help you in every way.

HOW TO AVOID FOUR COMMON WEBSITE RIP-OFFS

RIP-OFF #1: UNBELIEVABLY LOW PRICE. To some degree, all of us are attracted by low price because we want to work within budget. But some consultants use price as the bait for their false and misleading advertising. They offer a cheap price—even offering a free website—and then, once they're speaking with you, they pressure you into buying "add-ons". It's as if you were buying a car and found that the dealer was charging you extra for the tires and steering wheel. Having an online presence is not as cheap as some unethical companies would like you to believe.

RIP-OFF #2: CONTROL OF YOUR WEBSITE. This is a sad but very common rip-off. It has happened to a few of my own clients. A company will give you a low price but they control your website. When you go to make changes, you have to hire them for the changes.

RIP-OFF #3: NO REAL WORLD EXPERIENCE. It seems just about everyone is a social media consultant or website designer these days after building their family members website. Be careful because they usually don't know what they don't know since they don't have a lot of experience. Tony Robbins says, "The quickest way to success in anything is to find someone that is successful and model what they are doing". It is very important that you hire a consultant that makes their living from using the same strategies as they promote to their clients.

RIP-OFF #4: DOESN'T INCLUDE STRATEGIC SOLUTIONS. When I started Nashpreneur.com, I got it up to over $2,000 a month in just 90 days. One of the reasons why the site became successful very quickly is because it was built in a strategic way that most online companies don't know how to do. The consultants are typically more technical in nature instead of more strategic when they build their websites. It is very important that your consultant includes a strategic plan for not only how you will get prospects, but how to get them to convert into paying customers.

SIX COSTLY MISCONCEPTIONS ABOUT ONLINE MARKETING

MISCONCEPTION #1: Having a nice looking website is all a company needs.

Not true. Just because your site has a cute little flash video on the homepage or well-designed graphics, doesn't mean that it is setup to convert prospects into customers. Your website can be an asset to you and not a liability if you have a complete strategic marketing plan laid out ahead of time.

MISCONCEPTION #2: Build a website and they will come.

No. Just building a website and having it just sit there is really just an expensive business card. To reach and convert new customers, you will need to commit to ongoing marketing whether it be someone in your office that handles it, or another contracted company.

MISCONCEPTION #3: A small business website should be about your business.

Not true. This is a very important topic to cover. It isn't about you. It is about your prospect and what they want. I am not saying not to have things such as testimonials about you or your company, however, just about everything on your website should focus on the solution your prospects are looking for.

An example would be my own website, Nashpreneur.com. If you go there, it is all about helping small business owners. There is very little about me on the site except for the about me and work with Dave pages.

MISCONCEPTION #4: A small business website will not generate new business.

Not true. There are many ways to use a website to generate new business from pay per click to search engine optimization. My last client that hired me, heard me speak and went to my website that night to request more information from me. The key is using your website as a digital pinball machine so prospects and gets more information from you in various mediums.

MISCONCEPTION #5: The company that offers the lowest price is the company you should hire.

Maybe—but not always. I've seen so many problems arise from low ball website building companies. I suggest you hire with caution the company that quotes the cheapest price. The two most common problems are:

(1) The price may not cover exactly what is needed to have an effective website. Usually it is very limited.

(1) The price you see advertised may not be the price you pay. Many business professionals have learned that the low price they saw advertised lasted only until they got on the phone with the consultant. Then they were pressured into paying a lot more for a variety of add-ons. Some consultants may even break the law by using illegal bait and switch tactics.

MISCONCEPTION #6: Marketing online is expensive.

Not true. If your online marketing consultant will teach you how to use the website to build an automated marketing system, it is not expensive at all. Let me give you a quick example.

Many business owners go to local networking events and gather a bunch of business cards. What usually happens is they "may" follow up with a prospect once which usually isn't profitable since 81% of sales are made after the fifth contact.

What I teach my clients are to create education based marketing material to give away through email so that the prospect subscribes to the mailing list. Now a prospect can get more educated on your company and the solutions that you provide through your auto responder messages. By using your web presence in this way, you actually can make a lot more money than without having a web presence.

EIGHT MISTAKES TO AVOID WHEN CHOOSING AN ONLINE MARKETING CONSULTANT

MISTAKE #1: Choosing a web designer based on graphic design skills alone.

No question, your designer needs to have good graphic skills. But they also need something else. They need to have knowledge in areas such as social psychology and strategic thinking if you are looking for your web presence to convert prospects into customers.

MISTAKE # 2: Choosing a consultant based on low price.

Low price could be a problem in three ways: (1) Low price can be the bait that attracts your phone call. But once the consultant is talking with you, he pressures you into a much more expensive project. (2) Low price can be for a really stripped down site that might not be optimized for seo. Rarely does the consumer know about all the technical jargon and just doesn't know to ask the right questions.

MISTAKE #3: Choosing a consultant that only has book knowledge.

Your consultant should be very educated in the area of online marketing, however, be very careful that you don't hire someone with just book knowledge. Anyone can read an ebook or go to YouTube and watch videos on the subject then turn around and spout out what they just learned. It is an entirely other thing to have real world, in the trenches experience.

MISTAKE #4: Choosing a consultant who doesn't offer a money-back guarantee.

In my view, every online marketing company should be fully accountable for its work. And if you aren't pleased with the project in every way, you shouldn't have to pay for it. Period. Not all consultants offer a guarantee. Or, if they do, the guarantee may be "limited". Ask the consultant if he offers a money-back guarantee and then make sure the consultant includes his guarantee on his written quotation.

MISTAKE #5: Choosing a consultant without getting references from his or her other clients.

Any consultant can say anything about his past projects. And, sadly, some of what he says may not be true. Make sure you ask for references or read comments from current customers so you can depend on the consultant and his work.

THE IMPORTANCE OF VALUE AND PRICE

"Price is what you pay. Value and service is what you get."

When you select an online marketing consultant or designer, you'll choose from a wide variety of options and prices.

Not surprisingly, having your website built and online marketing plan created with professional, costs more than using a basic website builder.

If just having a nice business card type of website is all you want, then going with the cheapest service you can find might be all you need. No question, you can build a nice looking basic website—but the key word here is "basic". It will not become a digital pinball machine like I talk about in previous articles.

On the other hand, if you want a profitable website that converts prospects into customers—if you want it to look good and educate your prospects about your expertise without you being present—then you need to find a professional online marketing consultant. This means you need to find someone experienced with getting traffic to your site and also helping you design your sales funnel to convert prospects into customers.

Remember: "The bitterness of poor quality remains long after the sweetness of low price is forgotten.

DO YOU WANT A PROFESSIONAL LOOKING, CUSTOMER CONVERTING WEBSITE?

Which is more important to you: a professional website—or a professional and customer converting website? Yes, I assure you, there is a big difference.

There are several online marketing options out there and each has advantages and disadvantages. Some options will get you up and running. Other options will get you a few more bells and whistles. Still others will include virtually everything you need to not only have a professional website but have one that converts prospects into customers. And, to be sure, some are more expensive than others.

If all you want is a cheap, basic website—which you might find for around $19.95 per month—then I respectfully ask that you call another company.

But if you want to have a website that you are proud of and that's profitable—if you want to have an asset and not a liability, then you're invited to call me.

The software and the marketing tools that I use are some of the most powerful available today. I own all these tools for a good reason: More and more Nashville business professionals want the benefits that come from using a website to sell while they sleep.

Have you ever seen how dirty a little boy's pants get when he plays outdoors? If you have then you know you can brush off his pants and make him think they're clean. Or, if you want the job done right, you can machine wash them in hot water and detergent, and you'll know they're clean.

The same is true for your online marketing. You can hire someone or a service for $19.95 a month that will build you a website (aka "brush off") and make you think you have what you need to succeed. Or if you want the job done right, I'll build your website, give you the full marketing support that you need, and you'll have a competitive advantage over every other company in your industry.

So if you want a professional, customer converting website—if you're willing to invest in your business—you're invited to call me. You'll receive a written quotation, at no cost or obligation. And if you give us the go-ahead, you're further protected with my guarantee . . .

100% NO-RISK GUARANTEE

As the owner of Nashpreneur.com, I want you to be super-pleased—in fact, absolutely delighted—with the work my team and I do. So every job comes with our ironclad, risk-free guarantee. What does this mean? Simply this: If you aren't happy with our work, we'll work fix the problem. And if you still aren't pleased, you pay nothing. Not one cent. Many companies don't guarantee their work. But at Nashpreneur.com, nothing is more important than your complete and total satisfaction. We stand behind every project 100%. If you ever have any questions or concerns about our work, please call me right away at 615-796-0104.

"A Professional Customer Converting Website, or it's Free."

FOUR STEPS TO A PROFESSIONAL, CUSTOMER CONVERTING WEBSITE

If you're thinking about having a website built or want to use online marketing to generate more customers for your local business, I encourage you to follow these four steps:

Step #1: Make a commitment to yourself to get started. The longer you wait, the more likely your competitors might be listening to this message and takes action themselves.

Step #2: List your objectives. Do you want only a basic business card website, something you could do with a cheap service. Or do you want to use your website to further enhance all of your other marketing efforts to convert prospects to customers. Do you want to work with an honest, reputable company—or are you willing to risk working with the company that offers you the lowest price—knowing that the company might not be in business tomorrow.

Step #3: Ask questions. The way you learn about a company is to ask specific questions and listen carefully to the answers. Here are eight tough questions to ask an online marketing consultant before you agree to work with them:

1. What is your track record of success for your OWN websites?
2. What are some of your client success stories?
3. What training have you had in online marketing?
4. What is your experience with generating traffic to a website
5. How many products are or services have you sold online
6. Do you guarantee your work?

Step #4: Once you're satisfied that you're working with an honest, competent professional, invite him office and ask for a specific quotation in writing. A written quotation gives you the assurance you know exactly what your project will cost.

By following these four steps, you'll gain all the information you need to make an informed intelligent decision. If you want a quick, cheap website, there are many companies that can help you. Or you can use a service and build it yourself.

I'll be happy to answer your questions—provide you an estimate over the telephone—or come to your office and give you a free written quotation—without cost or obligation of any kind. To reach me, call 615-796-0104.

THANKS AGAIN!

. . . For reviewing my CONSUMER'S GUIDE TO SELECTING A PROFESSIONAL ONLINE MARKETING CONSULTANT FOR YOUR NASHVILLE BUSINESS.

I hope you found this information helpful.

If you have any questions or comments—of if you'd like me to give you an exact written quotation to build your website or handle your online marketing—please call me at 615-796-0104.

I've dedicated my business to consumer education and service. I'll be pleased to help you in every way. I look forward to your call. Thanks!

David Dutton
Nashpreneur.com

100 Great Places To Market Your Nashville Area Business

Section 1: Sponsorships.

1. Sponsor a meetup on meetup.com
2. Sponsor an event
3. Sponsor a Restaurant
4. Sponsor a charity event
5. Sponsor a podcast
6. Sponsor Local Chamber of Commerce Events
7. Sponsor Local Chamber of Commerce Website
8. Sponsor The Williamson County Human Resources Management Association
9. Sponsor Puckfest Hockey Tournaments
10. Sponsor Ronald Mcdonald House Golf Tournament
11. Sponsor your own tree at Hands On Nashville
12. Sponsor Solider Ride
13. Sponsor Musicians Corner
14. Sponsor Nashville Muse
15. Sponsor playing nashville
16. Sponsor Drula Camp Nashville
17. Sponsor Give Camp Nashville, TN

18.   Sponsor Middle TN Red Cross
19.   Sponsor Williamson County Event through Heritage Foundation including:
20.   Three Blind Vines
21.   Main Street Brew Fest
22.   Main Street Festival
23.   Tour of Homes
24.   Pumpkinfest
25.   Heritage Ball
26.   Dickens Christmas

Section 2: Advertising

List of local radio stations

27.   88.7 Way-FM Christian Music Radio
28.   90.3 WPLN Nashville Public Radio
29.   91.1 WRVU - Vanderbilt Alternative Rock
30.   97.9 WSIX –Big 98 Country
31.   99.7 WTN-Talk Radio
32.   100.1 WRLT Lightning 100
33.   01.1 WUBT The Beat
34.   05.1 WVRY Solid Gospel
35.   07.5 Clear Channel - The River
36.   360 WNAH - Gospel Country
37.   510 WLAC—News Radio

List of local newspapers

38.   City Paper
39.   Davidson A.M.
40.   MeterTennessee State University
41.   Nashville Business Journal
42.   Nashville Post
43.   Nashville Scene
44.   Tennessee Tribune
45.   Nashville Scene Tennessean
46.   Tennessee Register Tennessee Tribune

47. Vanderbilt Hustler Vanderbilt University
48. Leiper's Fork Life Franklin, TN and Brentwood, TN
49. Brentwood Journal
50. Fairview Observer
51. Journal of Spring Hill and Thompson's Station
52. Williamson Herald –Franklin, TN
53. Review Appeal- Franklin TN

List of school newspapers

54. Clarksville Austin Peay State University
55. Nashville Vanderbilt University

Section 3: Advertising Online

56. Advertise in Nashville Lifestyles Magazine
57. Advertise in local Chamber of Commerce Newsletter
58. Advertise on 365 Things to do in Downtown Nashville
59. Advertise on Manta.com
60. Advertise on Dexone.com
61. Advertise on Facebook
62. Advertise on Survival Insight
63. Advertise in Yelp
64. Advertise in Yahoo
65. Sign up for free online phone directory on yellowpages.com
66. Sign up for free online phone directory on yellowpagecity.com
67. Purchase ads in those directories
68. Advertise on HelloNashville.com

Section 4: Speaking

69. Speak at local networking groups
70. Create your own workshop or seminar
71. Create your own expo
72. Start your own meetup group

Section 5: Online Groups

List of Linkedin groups that talk about Nashville business related topics

73. Nashville Business Journal
74. Nashville Small Business Owners
75. Nashville Business Intelligence Group
76. Nashville Business Journal
77. Business Leadership team
78. Nashville Business Owners
79. Nashville Business Chamber
80. Nashville Post
81. Nashville Business Book Club
82. Nashville Network
83. Nashville Biz Golfers Network
84. Kiwanis Club of Nashville
85. BNI All Around Nashville
86. Nashville Local Business
87. Nashville Business Pulse
88. Nashville Business Magazine
89. BNI Franklin, TN Chapter
90. Cool Springs Business Society Franklin/Brentwood
91. Link IN! Williamson County, TN Franklin, TN
92. Start your own facebook group
93. Start your own LinkedIn group
94. Start your own google business page
95. Start your own blog

Section 6: Joint Ventures

96. Link your website to another business and ask them to do the same
97. Give away a free item with your website address and phone number
98. Cross promote other businesses products
99. Place other businesses add's on your thank you page
100. Swap business cards with other businesses
101. Survey Swap: Link a survey from one website and vice versa

Section 7: Networking Groups

102. Nashville Geek Breakfast
103. Women's Entrepreneurship Coffee
104. Innovation Nashville
105. Social Media Club Nashville
106. Nashville Geeks
107. Connect Nashville
108. Nashville SEO & Internet Marketing Group
109. Entrepreneur Center
110. Entrepreneurs Organization (Nashville Chapter)
111. PodCamp Nashville
112. Grow Nashville
113. WordPress Nashville
114. Nashville Tech
115. YP Nashville
116. CEO Nashville

Section 8: Referral Marketing

117. Join the 90-day Nashpreneur.com marketing challenge

Client Files:
From $300 to $11,800
In 11 Months

Because I know how hot the topic of marketing online is with local business professionals, I thought I would reach into my client files and share an interview I did with two Michigan guys who turned $300 a month into $11,800 in just 11 months using strategies that I taught them. Enjoy.

Visit www.nashpreneur.com/scd for the free recording

Bonus Interview With Jeff Livak Of Catapult Creative

This is a short interview with Jeff Livak. Jeff is a Nashpreneur who I met through my monthly marketing meetups. Jeff also did the branding for my Nashpreneurville event.

1. How did you become an expert on branding?

Graphic design has a broad range of disciplines but I always wanted to focus on branding. A few years into my career I got the opportunity to work at Monigle Associates, the largest independent branding firm in the nation. I worked alongside seasoned veterans in the industry where I honed my design skills and gained a much deeper understanding of how to develop the strategy that complex brands are built upon. I helped build identity packages for major industry leaders and got to see them rolled out in national and international markets. I've since started my own company, Catapult Creative, where I focus more of my time helping smaller and mid-sized companies refine their messaging and build a solid brand platform to grow on.

I fell in love with design early on in life. It has always been something I've been drawn to, even as a kid. I was always artistic and that gift was encouraged by my parents from the beginning. There are certain points in your life where seemingly small realizations become major turning points. I remember being fascinated by the logo on the Burton Air snowboard I got as a Christmas present in the early 90's. This was in my early teens as I was finding my own identity and this logo represented my new found passion for the sport (I grew up in Colorado where snow sports are a way of life). I studied the old snowboard company's catalogs and drew those logos over and over in my school notebooks. That passion and curiosity carried me through art classes, internships and eventually a Bachelor of Fine Arts with a concentration in Graphic Design.

I have always been intrigued by the skill of a logo designer to strike the delicate balance of communicating a complex message in such a simple and minimal way. I am fascinated by the hidden meanings and abstract representations contained in a great identity. The way a few lines can mean so much. How a symbol can convey two or three storylines. I love how an expertly handled font or color palette can evoke strong emotional responses that trigger fond memories or drive someone to behave in a certain way.

I find great joy in helping companies find their voice and establish a visual identity that allows them the opportunity to tell their story to their customers in a clear and consistent manner. It's incredible to educate our clients and watch them take the clarity they have gained about themselves and their brand and apply it, then see how the level of professionalism they convey is magnified by their new focused approach.

2. What are some of the top things Nashville professionals should consider when creating their brand?

1. Consistency. Consistency. Consistency.

There are several reasons why this is the most important concept in branding. Everything related to your business is considered a consumer touchpoint and should communicate the same message about your brand. From the quality of your business card to the type of sign in front of your store to the attitude of your employees, it all needs to communicate your brand essence.

Think of your brand as a building and each touchpoint is a brick. If the bricks are all laid in an intentional pattern and they all fit nicely together, the end result will be a solid structure that looks exactly as you intended it to look. Conversely, if those bricks are all different shapes and sizes where some are broken, some are missing, and some are just thrown on the pile, the end result is going to be a mess that nobody will recognize. You can't build a business on a shaky foundation.

2. Identity. Not Identical.

This relates back to the previous point about consistency. Every piece of marketing doesn't need to be identical to be consistently branded. A good brand should contain an entire suite of elements that can be used to varying degrees to "dial up" or "dial down" your brand. The system should be flexible enough to allow it to grow and evolve as the company evolves. A system that is too rigid is much more likely to be abandoned. Instead, establish a few basic rules for logo sizing and placement, color palette and font selections, then create guidelines, or an acceptable range, where these rules live. All applications of a well thought out brand should feel like part of the same family whether the branded elements are applied with maximum impact on your website's home page or reduced for minimal impact on a content-heavy sales sheet.

3. Control your message.

Control how you are perceived because it's almost impossible to break out of a negative brand image. You may have noticed how many "new" banks were suddenly in the market after the sub-prime lending debacle in recent years. They weren't new, they were banks whose name had been dragged through the mud with all of the negative publicity. Everything they had done to build their brands was shattered in seconds. Obviously there's a much deeper story to that example but the point is that a negative brand perception will ruin you very quickly. BP is another example of a brand that is spending a fortune trying to restore their brand image and regain their customers' trust after the Gulf spill.

4. Reward Loyalty.

Loyal customers are ambassadors for your brand. They are the ones who not only create a foundation of repeat business but they help communicate your brand essence to the rest of the market. Don't think brand loyalty is all that important? Try telling a Harley Davidson owner that there is a better motorcycle and that they should switch. Even if the other motorcycle is faster, more reliable and less expensive, Harley has done such an amazing job of creating brand loyalty that their customers are very unlikely to make the trade. Harley doesn't sell motorcycles; they sell a lifestyle—a beautifully branded lifestyle.

3. Is there a big difference in branding for big corporations versus a local business?

There are some slight differences. The scale by which the brand is implemented may vary greatly but the end goal remains the same. Rebranding an oil company with offices all over the world requires a more highly orchestrated rollout than a local bakery that wants to look more professional but both brand launches start by engaging the employees first, then rolling out messaging and visual systems that are focused and strategic. Companies, both large and small, need to study their market, find opportunities to stand out from their competition, and both must find a way to connect with their audience so that they can tell their story. At the end of the day, every brand is trying to make their audience remember them in a positive and intentional way to build an emotionally charged relationship.

In some ways I think branding is even more important for local businesses. For one, your marketing budget is most likely much smaller than that of a national corporation so you must make every dollar count. You can't afford to have an inconsistent or forgettable message when you have fewer opportunities to reach your customers.

Word-of-mouth is very important in a market like Nashville where people value the opinions of their neighbors and being trustworthy is a must-have quality. If you are not taking an active role in how your company is perceived by the local market, you risk being defined by your critics instead of your supporters.

4. What are your top 3 branding tips for Nashpreneurs?

1. Have a plan.

Take the time to understand your market and find the opportunities for you to stand out. Decide how you want your customers to think of you and develop a strategic plan to accomplish that. Select visual elements that reinforce your brand essence and collect them in a way that makes it easy to use in a consistent manner. Decide in advance how you plan to educate your customers about your brand and focus your marketing budget on the most effective channels to reach them. Be rigid enough in your plan to create a cohesive feel but flexible enough to allow your brand to adapt and grow and your business evolves.

2. Get your employees on board.

Get your employees excited about what you represent and involve them so they understand why it is important to live your brand promise. If you want your brand to be thought of as the most professional, courteous and friendly business in the local market, your employees are the ones that are responsible for making that a reality.

3. Tell your story.

Nobody can tell your story better than you can. Educate your audience about your values, your goals and your unique offerings. Give your customers a chance to get to know you and relate to you. Purchasing is largely an emotional decision, by sharing your story you are giving your customers an opportunity to build that emotional bond with you.

5. What are the top most embarrassing mistakes you see people make?

Over-design.

It seems to be human nature to make things more complicated than they need to be and design is no different. When it comes to branding, marketing and website design, one of the most common mistakes is to over-design. Too many bells, whistles and flashing lights clutter the page and dilutes the message. If everything is important then nothing is important. Decide what your message is and design in a way that enhances that message. Strip away all of the decoration and visual clutter that does not serve a clear purpose in communicating that message. Apple is the example most commonly used to illustrate how effective a brand can be when using this principle.

Presenting an inconsistent message.

Inconsistency creates confusion and confusion is the enemy of decision. It also makes you look disorganized. The goal of your brand is to clearly communicate your unique offerings and reinforce your brand promise. Your messaging should be written in a voice that is consistent with your brand's personality (friendly and approachable, serious and professional, etc). Consistency creates trust, trust creates loyalty, and loyalty creates brand ambassadors.

Overpromising and under delivering.

This is a basic rule of business that is often violated by ambitious business owners that are either trying to appear bigger than they are or have not created a culture within their company that supports their grandiose brand promise. To solve this, be sure not to overcommit and work to create a company culture that is consistent with your promises by engaging your employees. Then do what you say you're going to do.

Not thinking strategically.

Unfocused marketing, inconsistent messaging, not listening to the customers' needs, and lack of vision all waste valuable time and resources. They also make it look like you're uncertain about how to run your business. If you don't know what you're doing, it's hard to convince your customers that your product is reliable and they should trust you.

6. When hiring someone to design a logo or an entire brand, what should a person ask?

I would encourage people to think bigger about what they are trying to accomplish when they say they need a logo. While your logo is the most obvious and visible element in your brand package, it can't fully communicate everything that you stand for. When it is supported by complementary elements like a defined color palette, resolved typographic hierarchy, structural guidelines, unique photographic style, support graphics and a consistent voice, the personality of the brand really comes to life. Every company has a logo but the companies who stand out do so with a cohesive visual identity.

Most importantly, you should ask to see the samples of the designer's previous work. Their portfolio will give you the best indication of their talents and whether their unique style is a match for your business. Not every designer will suit your needs, shop around and find someone who resonates with you.

Then I would ask any potential designer a few simple questions. Their answers will reveal how deeply they understand your needs.

1. What is your process?

Get some insight about how the designer plans to solve your problem. How much research do they do before they start designing? How many concepts will they provide? How many revisions are allowed in the quoted price? What is the payment schedule? What happens if there are major changes to the scope or if the project gets cancelled or postponed for any reason?

2. What are the deliverables (What can I expect to receive)?

Make sure you are clear about what you need and what you expect from the designer. If you need business cards, PowerPoint presentations, advertising, newsletters or anything else, be sure to include it in the bid. Will you be needing any guidelines written to help you maintain consistency?

Be certain you are receiving artwork in all the formats you will need. For example, as part of our identity packages we deliver logo files in vector and raster formats that solve for every type of potential use so you will always have the right file for printed or digital applications as well as restricted uses like screen printing, embroidery, black-and-white newspaper ads, signage, etcetera. Depending on the scope, we typically design several application templates and provide final artwork for each. Then we wrap up the project by delivering a set of guidelines that show exactly how everything is intended to be used by your internal design team, advertising agencies and vendors. Brand Standards Guidelines are an important way to protect your investment by clearly outlining the basic principles that your brand is built upon to ensure high standards are maintained for the life of the brand.

3. What happens after the identity is designed?

Will your designer be there to help you if you have any issues or are you on your own as soon as the last invoice has been paid? Is the designer capable of helping you implement your new brand system? If you need help rolling out your new identity or marketing your business, is this something your designer is capable of offering?

Think through how you intend to use your new brand and look for partnerships that will add long-term value. Some full-service agencies are a "Jack-of-all-trades, master of none", while others do a great job in many different disciplines. Some designers are specialists in one area of expertise but have relationships with experts with complementary skillsets as well. Again, find the designer or group of designers that feels like the best fit for your needs.

4. Agree on a Timeline.

There are several phases you and your designer must go through to land on a final design. Be sure to inform your designer if you have a specific date you need to have everything completed by and make sure they can meet that deadline. Finding the best solution is not a linear process. Designers need time to research your market and explore potential themes, then conceptualize, revise, edit, rework, prepare and present. Oftentimes the best ideas need time to incubate so a project may get set aside for a few days to allow the subconscious to work things out. My best ideas usually come to me in the shower or some other inconvenient time while away from my desk.

One of the best quotes I've ever heard about the design process was from one of my professors who said "a design is never done, it's simply due." As designers we will tinker and try to improve our work up until the last minute so set realistic timelines that will give your designer ample time to fully explore the potential of their concepts but make sure there is a deadline for each phase of the project so things continue to progress in a timely manner.

If the designer is any good, you're probably not their only client. Make sure your project fits within their existing workload and they confirm that they can meet your deadline.

Pricing can vary greatly from designer to designer. Some prefer to use a fixed pricing plan, some prefer to provide customs bids based on your specific needs. Your budget will often dictate how much time is spent on each phase of the project and how many revisions are allowed. Make sure you're on the same page with what is expected to avoid any surprises or hard feelings. An experienced designer should have all of these concerns clearly outlined in their bid.

Most importantly, get everything you agree upon in writing.

About Jeff Livak

Jeff Livak is the owner of Catapult Creative here in Nashville and specializes in comprehensive branding systems and website design for small to mid-sized businesses. Jeff graduated from Colorado State University in 2003 with a Bachelor of Fine Arts degree in Graphic Design. A Colorado native, Jeff lived and worked in Denver and Los Angeles before relocating to Nashville with his wife and new baby girl. Besides being consumed by design, he enjoys skiing, snowboarding, cycling, running, painting and music. You can reach him at jeff@catapultcreative.com.

Will You Do Me
A Favor?

You can ask each contributing author what I said the goal is of each chapter and they will tell you that I wanted a local professional to be able to pick up this book, flip to any chapter, and leave a better business professional.

I sincerely hope that we have accomplished that for you.

We and other entrepreneurs would like to know what you think about the Ultimate Nashville Business Guide. All you need to do is call **1-214-702-5704 extension 123456** and follow the recorded instructions that you hear.

I am going to take the positive comments I get and post them on Nashpreneur. com and on a call in line so others can listen to them as well.

You might even become slightly famous by leaving your thoughts on the book since a lot of people locally will be checking it out. If you leave me your email address as well, I will even send you a bonus gift to show my appreciation.

Again, the number is **1-214-702-5704 extension 123456.**

I really appreciate you helping me out as we help Nashville business professionals grow their business.

Take care and God bless

David Dutton

CPSIA information can be obtained at www.ICGtesting.com
Printed in the USA
LVOW120830211112

308285LV00005B/1/P